Mars Exploration
Fact and Fantasy

Bruce LaFontaine

DOVER PUBLICATIONS, INC.
Mineola, New York

ABOUT THE AUTHOR

Bruce LaFontaine is the writer and illustrator of thirty-five non-fiction children's books. He specializes in the subject areas of history, science, transportation, and architecture for middle readers, ages eight through twelve. Mr. LaFontaine's published works include *Modern Experimental Aircraft*, *Famous Buildings of Frank Lloyd Wright*, *Great Inventors and Inventions*, and many others. His book, *Exploring the Solar System*, published in 1999, was selected by *Astronomy* magazine as one of the twenty-one best astronomy books for children. In the same year, Mr. LaFontaine was profiled in *Something About the Author*, a hardcover publication featuring prominent authors and illustrators in the field of children's literature. Mr. LaFontaine served as a staff sergeant in the United States Air Force during the Vietnam era. He has worked in the Rochester, New York area as a writer, illustrator, and art director for twenty-five years.

Published in Canada by General Publishing Company, Ltd., 895 Don Mills Road, 400-2 Park Centre, Toronto, Ontario M3C 1W3.
Published in the United Kingdom by David & Charles, Brunel House, Forde Close, Newton Abbot, Devon TQ12 4PU.

Bibliographical Note

Mars Exploration: Fact and Fantasy is a new work, first published by Dover Publications, Inc., in 2002.

DOVER *Pictorial Archive* SERIES

International Standard Book Number: 0-486-41864-2

Manufactured in the United States of America
Dover Publications, Inc., 31 East 2nd Street, Mineola, N.Y. 11501

INTRODUCTION

Mars, the Red Planet. This dramatic image has gripped both the public imagination and riveted the attention of scientific investigators through the ages. Even before the invention of the telescope, Mars' distinct reddish hue was visible to the naked eye, and was recorded by the early astronomers who observed it. The ancient civilizations of Egypt and Greece associated this celestial body with war and death. The Romans named it "Mars," after their god of war.

In the late nineteenth century, the planet finally came under much closer scrutiny by astronomers using powerful telescopes. The sensational observations made by Giovanni Schiaparelli in 1877 and Percival Lowell in 1895 catapulted the Red Planet into public prominence. Their reports of "canals" on the Martian surface began a cycle of intense scientific inquiry and speculative science-fiction literature that continues to this day. These seemingly contrary endeavors have actually served as mutual inspiration: new factual information about Mars has fired the imaginations of novelists, while the fascinating and inventive stories about the planet have fueled the engine of science.

Eminent science fiction authors such as H. G. Wells, Arthur C. Clarke, and Ray Bradbury have spun exciting and thoughtful tales about Mars, but the factual data accumulated over the past thirty-five years is equally compelling. Beginning in 1965, exploratory robot spacecraft launched by the American space agency NASA began a photographic survey of Mars. The Mariner series of Mars probes sent back hundreds of images that were taken from only a few thousand miles above the planet. In addition to revealing remarkable details of the Martian landscape never before seen, the planet was found to possess spectacular geological features that stunned both the public and the scientific community. Its ancient, cratered surface is punctuated by gigantic extinct volcanoes and immense canyon systems far greater than any of their earthly counterparts. In 1976, the Viking spacecraft were the first vehicles from Earth to soft-land on the plains of Mars, relaying detailed pictures of the surrounding rock-strewn desert terrain.

During the 1990s there was a steady stream of robot probes sent to Mars. The Pathfinder spacecraft landed on the planet in 1997, and its six-wheeled vehicular companion, the Sojourner Rover, explored and examined nearby rock formations. The Mars Global Surveyor spacecraft has been in orbit around the planet since 1997, and continues to send back high-resolution color images as it maps the entire Martian surface. Probes such as these have suggested that Mars was once a warmer planet with liquid water on its surface. They have uncovered evidence of flood plains, river channels, and even an ancient ocean shoreline, all dating from early in the planet's history. How Mars lost its hospitable Earth-like environment and became the harsh and barren world of today is one among many of the important

(continued)

questions to be answered by future Mars missions. Finally, is there or was there ever life on Mars? Such questions as these lead inexorably to one of the fundamental scientific puzzles: Are we alone in the universe?

A meteorite discovered in 1984 on the ice fields of Antarctica, and eventually identified as originating from Mars, hints at the possibility that life did indeed once exist on the planet. A number of increasingly sophisticated robot spacecraft are scheduled to explore the planet over the next fifteen years. NASA has proposed to launch a mobile scientific laboratory as early as 2007, while a small Scout mission is planned for the same year. These and other NASA projects are leading up to a Mars expedition with a human crew sometime between 2015 and 2020, but it's possible that unexpected discoveries about the planet made by the robot probes may hasten this timetable. Or it may be that breakthroughs in propulsion technology will prompt an earlier manned mission. Whenever this first historic visit occurs, the whole world will be watching. And whether or not the mystery of life on Mars is ever resolved, the Red Planet will continue to exert a strong pull on the human imagination.

1. MARS, ROMAN GOD OF WAR

Astronomy, the science of observing, measuring, and describing objects in the sky, began 3,500 years ago in the ancient civilization of Mesopotamia. Lacking telescopes or other instruments, these early astronomers relied on the naked eye to study the night sky. Their primary scrutiny focused on seven celestial bodies: the sun, the moon and the five "wandering stars" that we now know as the planets Mercury, Venus, Mars, Jupiter, and Saturn. They discovered that these objects moved in regular patterns, unlike the multitude of other fixed stars in the sky. The term "planet" is from the Greek word *planetes*, meaning *wanderer*.

Mars stood out among these "wanderers" due to its reddish color, visible even to the naked eye. The Sumerians regarded the planet as a symbol of blood and war. Mars was known by many names among the ancients including *Nergal* by the Babylonians, *Harmakhis* by the Egyptians, and *Tui* by English/Germanic peoples. The classical Greek civilization called the planet *Ares*, after their war god. The Romans gave the planet its current name, *Mars*, after their own god of war. *Mars* is shown above seated on his throne and surrounded by weapons of the ancient world.

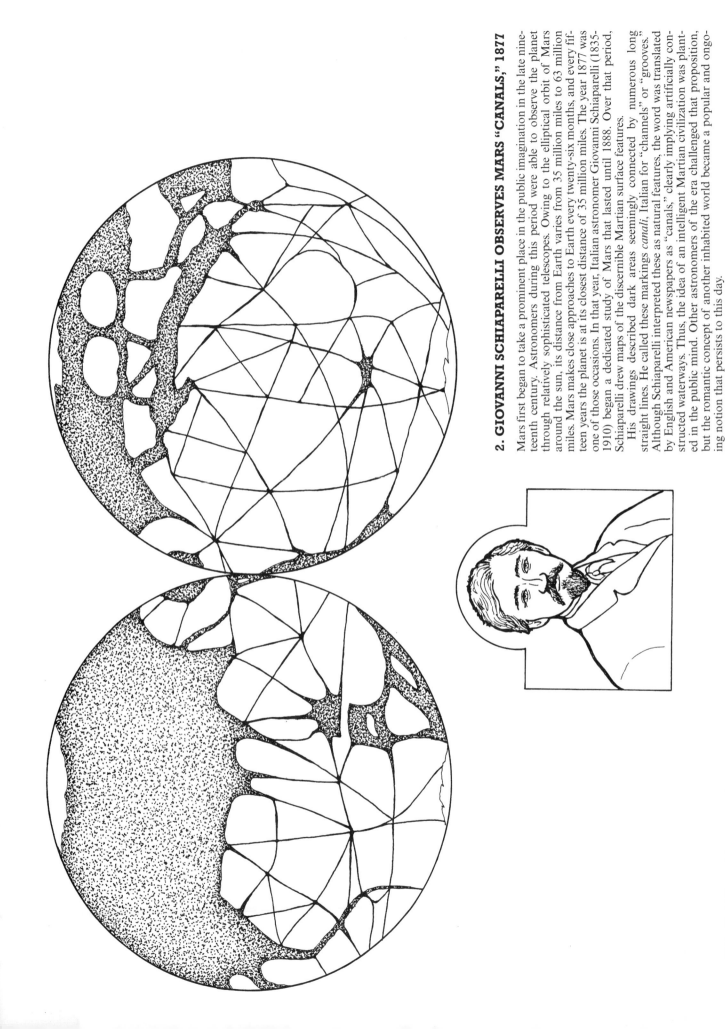

2. GIOVANNI SCHIAPARELLI OBSERVES MARS "CANALS," 1877

Mars first began to take a prominent place in the public imagination in the late nineteenth century. Astronomers during this period were able to observe the planet through relatively sophisticated telescopes. Owing to the elliptical orbit of Mars around the sun, its distance from Earth varies from 35 million miles to 63 million miles. Mars makes close approaches to Earth every twenty-six months, and every fifteen years the planet is at its closest distance of 35 million miles. The year 1877 was one of those occasions. In that year, Italian astronomer Giovanni Schiaparelli (1835-1910) began a dedicated study of Mars that lasted until 1888. Over that period, Schiaparelli drew maps of the discernible Martian surface features.

His drawings described dark areas seemingly connected by numerous long straight lines. He called these markings *canali*, Italian for "channels" or "grooves." Although Schiaparelli interpreted these as natural features, the word was translated by English and American newspapers as "canals," clearly implying artificially constructed waterways. Thus, the idea of an intelligent Martian civilization was planted in the public mind. Other astronomers of the era challenged that proposition, but the romantic concept of another inhabited world became a popular and ongoing notion that persists to this day.

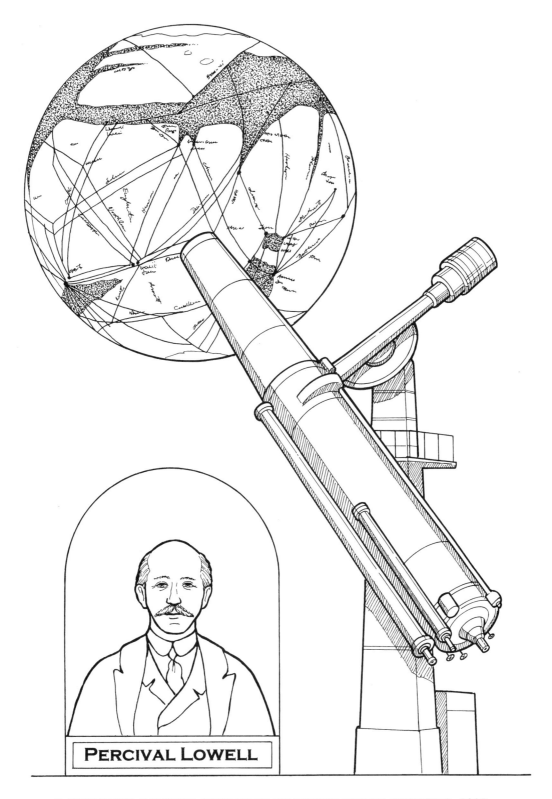

3. PERCIVAL LOWELL OBSERVES MARTIAN CANAL SYSTEMS, 1895

The speculation about an intelligent civilization on Mars received its greatest boost from amateur American astronomer Percival Lowell (1855-1916). Educated at Harvard University as a mathematician, Lowell chose astronomy as his career, focusing particularly on the study of Mars. As a member of a wealthy Boston family, he was able to finance construction of his own observatory in 1894 in the mountains of northern Arizona, near Flagstaff. Beginning in 1895, he launched a dedicated program of study and observation of Mars that continued for 15 years.

Using the 24-inch Clark refracting telescope, a powerful instrument for its day, Lowell observed what he described as "canals," connected by oases that covered the surface of the planet. He conjectured that a Martian civilization had con-

structed this elaborate planet-wide system of aqueducts to transport water from the melting polar ice caps to the dry equatorial regions of Mars. He drew elaborate maps of the canals and their interconnecting oasis "pumping stations." He also proposed that the changing dark patterns observed on Mars were actually large areas of vegetation that grew and receded with the Martian seasons.

In three books that received widespread public and scientific attention, Lowell explained his ideas about Mars. The first, *Mars*, was published in 1895; the next, *Mars and Its Canals*, in 1906; and the last, *Mars as the Abode of Life*, in 1908. Although many astronomers of the day disagreed with Lowell's assertions, his books further strengthened the public fascination with Mars and its possible inhabitants.

4.—5. SPECULATIVE VIEW OF MARTIAN CANAL PUMPING STATION

Shown above is an interpretation of Percival Lowell's ideas describing the complex system of canals and pumping stations contained in his books about Mars.

10. ARTHUR C. CLARKE WRITES *THE SANDS OF MARS*, 1952

One of the first books written by prolific and prophetic science-fiction novelist Arthur C. Clarke, *The Sands of Mars* also deals with human colonization of the red planet. It is distinguished by a fictional concept introduced in the story that has now become sound scientific theory. His book describes how colonists transform Mars into an earth-like planet through a process we now call "terraforming." The Mars settlers in Clarke's book discover a native plant and an indigenous Martian animal, both of which exist only in small numbers and remote locations. The vegetation is able to extract, store, and release oxygen from the sandy soil of Mars, while by eating the plant, the animal obtains enough oxygen to survive in the planet's thin atmosphere. The plants only grow in narrow equatorial regions and are not plentiful enough to oxygenate the entire planet. In order to increase the temperature of Mars and allow the plants to grow widely across the surface, the colonists ignite a thermonuclear reaction on the Martian moon Phobos, transforming it into a mini-sun. Warmed by this new sun, the atmosphere of Mars eventually thickens with oxygen and becomes more earth-like. Scientific plans for terraforming Mars into a habitable planet are now under serious consideration by today's scientists, another twist wherein science has been guided by speculative fiction.

11. *THE WAR OF THE WORLDS* RADIO BROADCAST, 1938, AND MOTION PICTURE, 1953

H. G. Wells's *The War of the Worlds* was adapted into a live radio broadcast in 1938, and a technicolor Hollywood film in 1953.

The radio version was created by Orson Welles for his popular Mercury Theater radio program and broadcast on October 30, 1938. Although the show was introduced as a dramatization of the novel, it was delivered in a realistic documentary style. Many listeners who did not hear the introduction thought that they were listening to an actual live news report of a Martian invasion of earth. Welles had moved the location of the story from Victorian England to a contemporary setting in the small town of Grover's Mill, New Jersey. Frightened residents in the area swamped police stations with phone calls about the destruction being reported on the radio. The *New York Times* received over 800 phone calls. At the conclusion of the broadcast, Welles reminded the audience that it was just a radio play and wished them a happy Halloween. Nevertheless, it caused widespread panic among gullible radio listeners.

In 1953, *The War of the Worlds* was adapted into a thoughtful, well-made Hollywood film. The setting of the invasion was once again changed, this time from England to the mountains near Los Angeles, California. The Martian fighting machines were also updated and redesigned as manta ray-winged flying craft able to discharge deadly red heat rays from a central projector "eye" and powerful green disintegrator beams from their wingtips. Impervious to the tanks and artillery sent to stop them, the Martians advanced on Los Angeles. Even an atomic bomb dropped by a high-flying aircraft could not stop the invaders. One of the most famous scenes in the film depicts Los Angeles city hall being destroyed by a Martian fighting machine, one of the many special effects that won the film an Academy Award. As in the novel, the Martians are finally stopped by the lowly cold germ to which their bodies have no resistance.

12. *INVADERS FROM MARS*,
DIRECTED BY WILLIAM CAMERON MENZIES, 1953

Science-fiction films were in full bloom during the 1950s, benefiting from the enormous progress of science and technology made during World War II. The postwar world had such wonders as jet aircraft, rocket-powered missiles, and the atomic bomb. In 1957, the space age began with the launching of *Sputnik*, the world's first artificial satellite. These scientific advancements were perfect raw material for science fiction and fantasy films and literature.

One of the most stylish and frightening films of this era was *Invaders from Mars*, directed by William Cameron Menzies. He had also directed an earlier science-fiction movie classic, *Things to Come*, the 1936 film version of an H. G. Wells novel. He was better known, however, for his work as a daring and innovative production designer on such films as *Gone with the Wind* (1939) and *The Thief of Bagdad* (1940). His talent was clearly evident in the visual design of *Invaders from Mars*. The story is told from the perspective of a ten-year-old boy. To heighten the sense of danger and threat, the oversized sets were photographed from a steep angle, giving the illusion that they are closing in on the young hero.

The plot follows the boy's awakening during the night to witness a spaceship landing behind a hill in his backyard. The boy tells his parents, who go outside to investigate. When they return, they have changed. No longer the kind and caring parents that he knew, they have become instead cold and violent. Soon, many of the townspeople have also changed. They have been kidnapped by the Martian invaders and subjected to a mind-controlling surgical implant. The boy is finally able to convince a few adults of what is happening and the army is called in to stop the invasion. They discover the Martian lair beneath a sandpit and encounter the golden-headed, tentacled Martian leader and his eight-foot-tall green soldier-slaves. A battle ensues in which the Martian ship is destroyed as it attempts to take off. All is well until the scene dissolves back to the boy's bedroom. He awakens; it had all been a dream. But then he hears a sound outside his window and sees a spaceship again descending behind the hill. Nightmare or reality, *Invaders from Mars* proved to be a powerful science-fiction film classic.

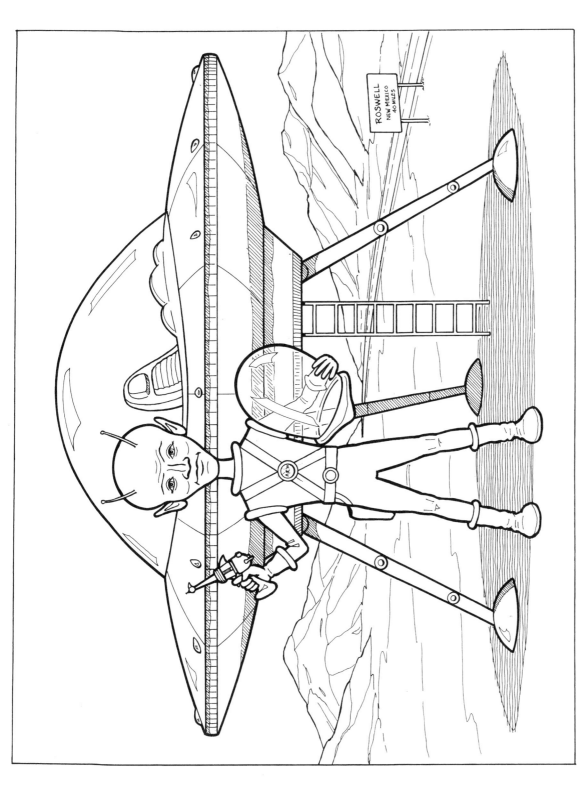

13. LITTLE GREEN MAN FROM MARS, 1950s

Another byproduct of the 1950s preoccupation with space-age technology and science fiction was the explosion of public interest in "Flying Saucers." They were first described in 1947 by businessman Kenneth Arnold as he piloted his private plane over the mountains of Washington state. He reported seeing a formation of disc-shaped craft flying at high speed. Soon, more sightings of these "flying saucers" by pilots, policemen, and ordinary citizens filled the nation's newspapers. Also called unidentified flying objects or "UFOs," they captured the public's imagination. Investigations could not determine whether they were really extraterrestrial spaceships, secret advanced military aircraft, natural phenomena, or just plain hoaxes. Flying saucers piloted by "Little Green Men from Mars" became the subject of widespread speculation in books, magazines, films, television shows, cartoons, and comic books. Interest in UFOs remains strong to this day, but the image of the "Little Green Man from Mars" has changed. People who claim to have been abducted by these space visitors describe them as "…gray-skinned, less than four feet tall, with large heads and huge black teardrop-shaped eyes." These beings are popularly referred to as "small grays" within the UFO investigation community. Whether they really exist and are in fact aliens from another world is a question only time will answer.

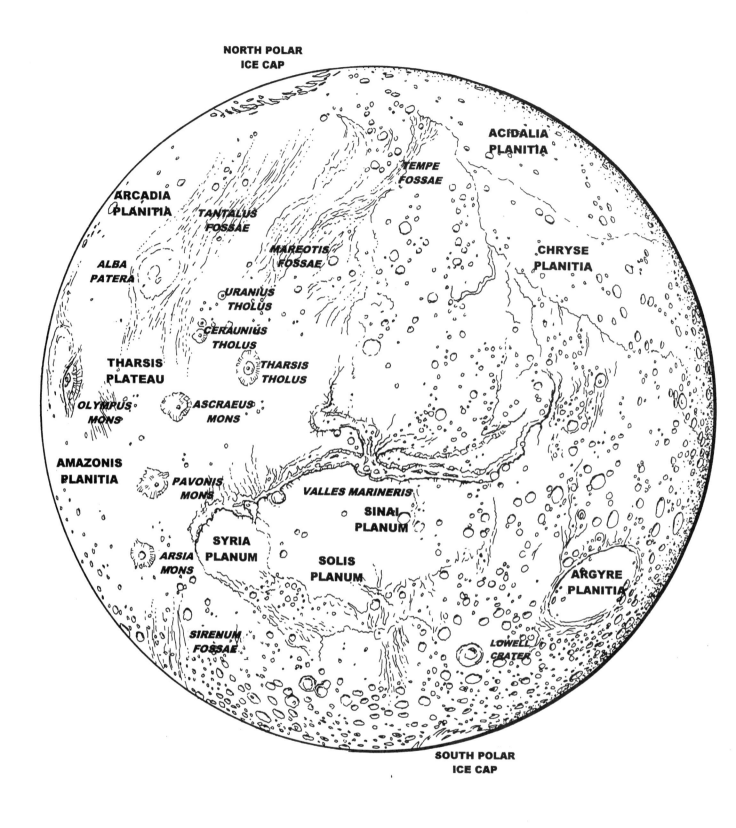

NORTH POLAR ICE CAP

ACIDALIA PLANITIA

TEMPE FOSSAE

ARCADIA PLANITIA

TANTALUS FOSSAE

MAREOTIS FOSSAE

CHRYSE PLANITIA

ALBA PATERA

URANIUS THOLUS

CERAUNIUS THOLUS

THARSIS PLATEAU

THARSIS THOLUS

OLYMPUS MONS

ASCRAEUS MONS

AMAZONIS PLANITIA

PAVONIS MONS

VALLES MARINERIS

SINAI PLANUM

SYRIA PLANUM

SOLIS PLANUM

ARGYRE PLANITIA

ARSIA MONS

SIRENUM FOSSAE

LOWELL CRATER

SOUTH POLAR ICE CAP

18. MARS HEMISPHERE CENTERED ON *VALLES MARINERIS*

This view of Mars shows some of the most spectacular geological formations on the planet. The immense canyon system, *Valles Marineris*, meanders across the center of the hemisphere. On the left side of the planet, the elevated Tharsis Plateau contains a series of massive extinct volcanoes, dominated by gigantic *Olympus Mons*. Two other geological features are also in this region. *Alba Patera* is an upraised volcanic dome caused by the internal pressure of molten lava. Long, ragged fissures in the crust of the planet are called *fossae*. They are cracks caused by internal volcanic and seismic activity. Mars has polar ice caps mainly composed of frozen carbon dioxide; the northern polar cap is significantly larger than the southern ice cap.

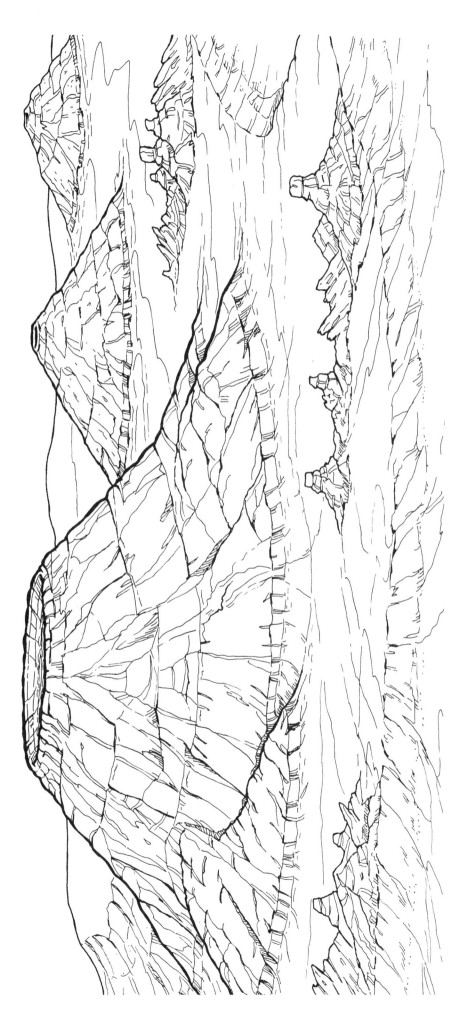

19. THARSIS PLATEAU VOLCANOES: *ARSIA MONS, PAVONIS MONS, ASCRAEUS MONS*

The northern hemisphere of Mars contains a large highland plain called the Tharsis Plateau or "bulge." It is 2,500 miles wide and roughly 6 miles higher than the surrounding landscape. Three extinct volcanoes of immense proportions rise along a crescent-shaped mountainous ridge on the plateau. Nine other smaller volcanoes also dot the surface of the Tharsis Bulge.

The three largest volcanoes are named *Arsia Mons, Pavonis Mons,* and *Ascraeus Mons.* They are classified as "shield" volcanoes owing to their roughly circular shield-like shape. The most massive of these is *Ascraeus Mons* at 35,904 feet high and 250 miles in diameter at its base. Next in size is *Arsia Mons* standing 29,462 feet high, equivalent to earth's tallest mountain, Mt. Everest. *Arsia Mons* has the largest caldera of any of the great Martian volcanoes. A caldera is the sunken crater at the summit of an extinct or dormant volcano. The

caldera of *Arsia Mons* is 68 miles in diameter and 3,000 feet deep. The last of these towering giants is *Pavonis Mons,* which rises to an altitude of 22,915 feet.

The Tharsis Plateau and its volcanoes were most likely created by a tremendous upwelling of molten rock, or magma, from the core of Mars. This probably occurred several billion years ago when Mars was a very geologically active planet. There is also a theory that the Tharsis Bulge was caused by the gigantic impact of a large asteroid or planetesimal—a small planet—on the opposite side of Mars. This collision reverberated through the planet's core causing a bulge on the surface. Evidence to support this theory comes from the existence of a huge impact crater, the Hellas basin, on the side of Mars opposite the Tharsis Plateau.

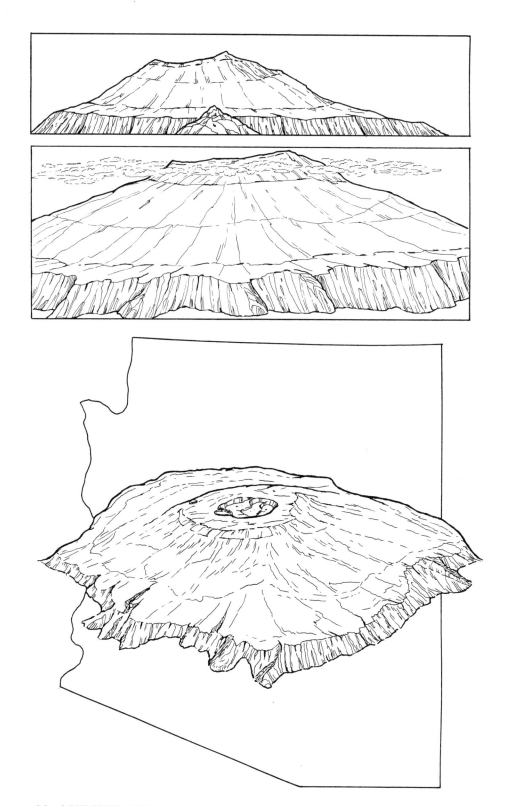

20. *OLYMPUS MONS,* LARGEST MOUNTAIN IN THE SOLAR SYSTEM

The greatest of the giant shield volcanoes of Mars rises from the Amazonis Planitia region. It is aptly named *Olympus Mons,* "Mt. Olympus," and dwarfs any other mountains on Earth or Mars. This extinct volcanic cone reaches an incredible altitude of 81,840 feet! With a diameter of 374 miles, *Olympus Mons* could cover the state of Arizona. Its huge caldera is over 50 miles wide. The base of the mountain is ringed by cliffs that rise almost vertically to a height of 22,000 feet above the surrounding plain. The rest of the mountain continues upward from that escarpment. By comparison, the largest shield volcano on earth, Mauna Loa in Hawaii, stands just 33,254 feet high; however, two thirds of its bulk is submerged beneath the Pacific Ocean.

There are several theories as to why Martian mountains are so much higher than those on Earth. Primarily, the lower gravity of a small planet like Mars has allowed these immense rock piles to grow without collapsing under their own tremendous weight. Additionally, lava flows at a single site on Mars lasted much longer than on Earth. The Earth's crust is composed of moving tectonic plates that have drifted over millions of years. This continual movement pulls volcanic hotspots into new locations around the planet. Crustal movement on Mars ceased billions of years ago, allowing huge buildups of erupted lava to form at a specific site. One of the most awe-inspiring sights in history will greet astronauts exploring Mars when they experience the first close-up view of the colossal grandeur of *Olympus Mons.*

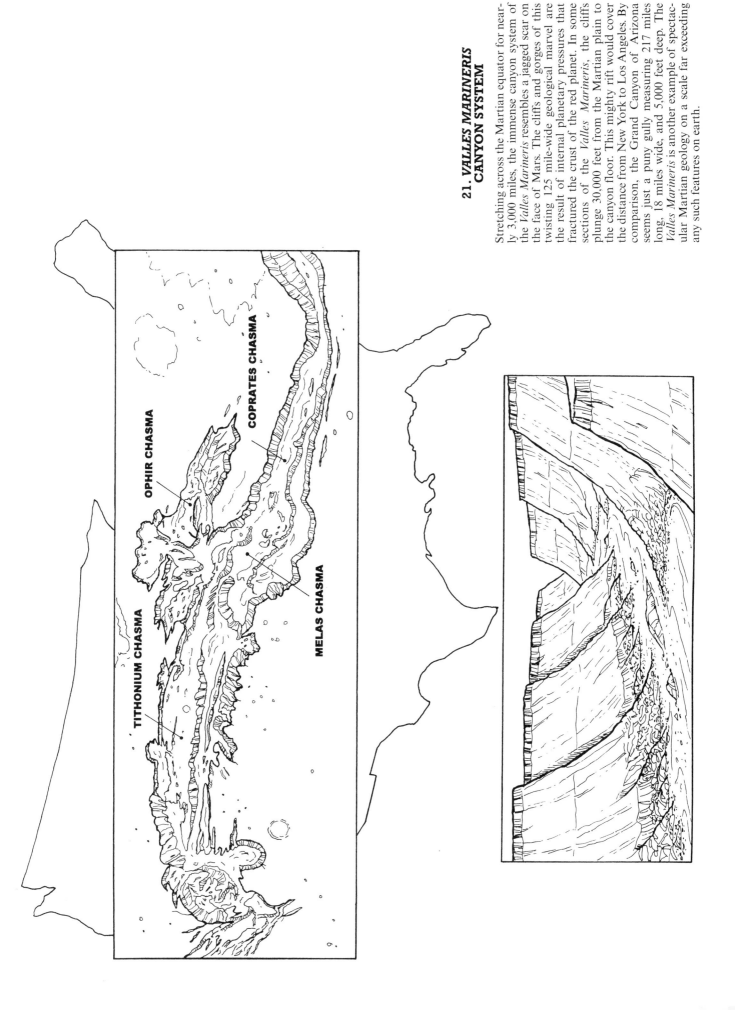

21. *VALLES MARINERIS* CANYON SYSTEM

Stretching across the Martian equator for near-ly 3,000 miles, the immense canyon system of the *Valles Marineris* resembles a jagged scar on the face of Mars. The cliffs and gorges of this twisting 125 mile-wide geological marvel are the result of internal planetary pressures that fractured the crust of the red planet. In some sections of the *Valles Marineris*, the cliffs plunge 30,000 feet from the Martian plain to the canyon floor. This mighty rift would cover the distance from New York to Los Angeles. By comparison, the Grand Canyon of Arizona seems just a puny gully measuring 217 miles long, 18 miles wide, and 5,000 feet deep. The *Valles Marineris* is another example of spectac-ular Martian geology on a scale far exceeding any such features on earth.

OPHIR CHASMA

COPRATES CHASMA

TITHONIUM CHASMA

MELAS CHASMA

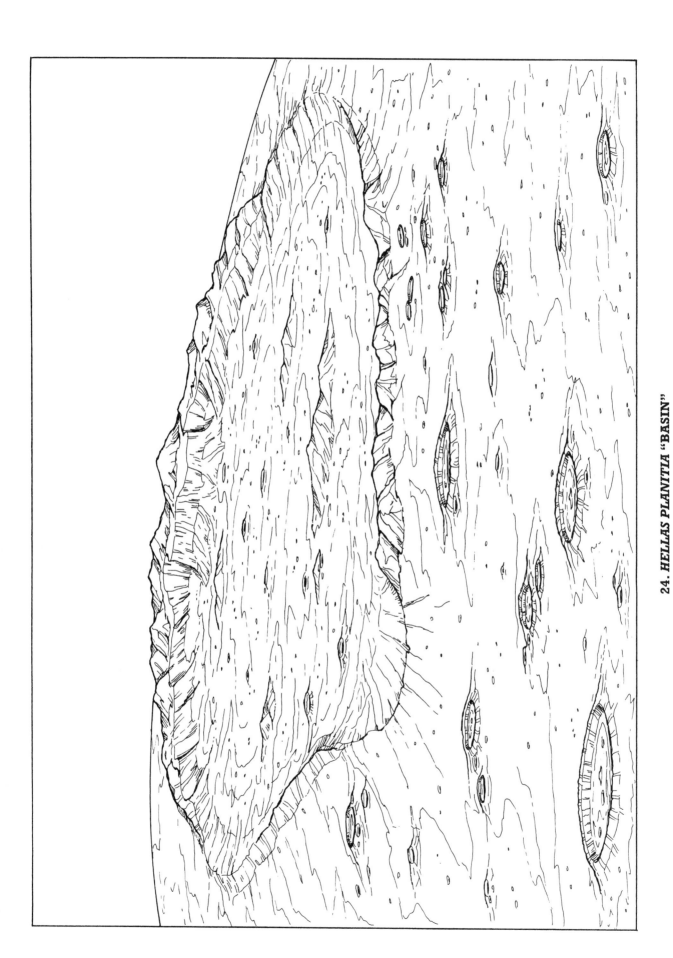

24. *HELLAS PLANITIA* "BASIN"

The force of the impact explosion that created the Hellas Basin crater also ejected billions of tons of molten rock into the atmosphere. This material settled back down to form a ring of moun- tains around the outer edge of the crater. In some places these mountainous crater walls descend 31,000 feet to the floor of the basin, an enormously deep depression in the surface of Mars.

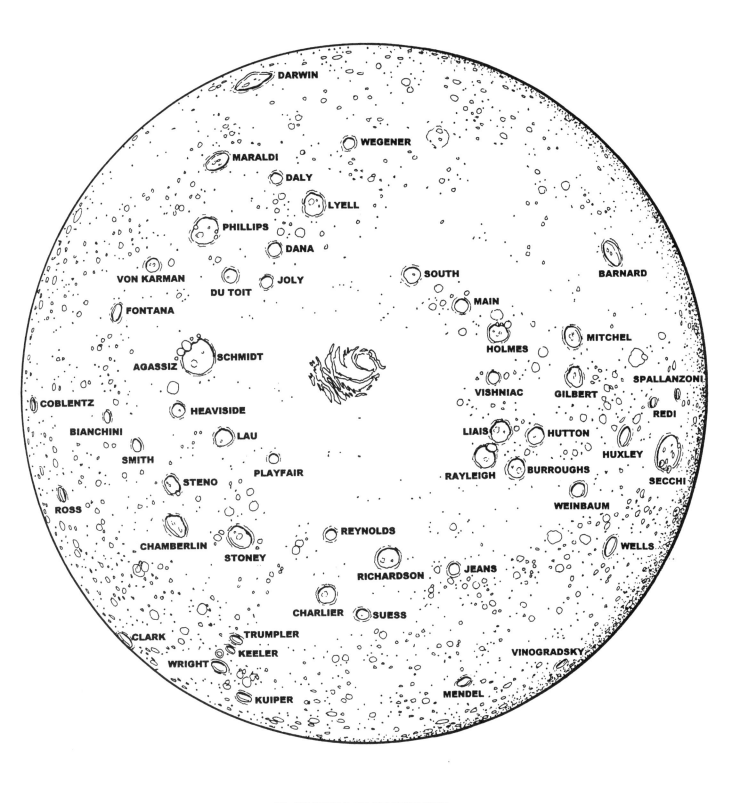

25. SOUTH POLAR ICE CAP

As seen in this global view centered on the Martian south pole, the southern ice cap is normally much smaller than its northern cousin. It is composed primarily of frozen carbon dioxide with a small quantity of frozen water ice. The permanent ice cap is 215 miles in diameter, but on rare occasions in midwinter, the seasonal ice cap can grow to a size of 2,400 miles. The temperature of this region of Mars never rises above minus 150 degrees centigrade (Celsius).

Also plainly evident from this view of Mars is the heavily cratered southern hemisphere of the planet. Scientists believe that the vast difference in the amount of cratering between the northern and southern hemispheres of Mars is due to the greater amount of volcanic activity in the north. The giant volcanoes of the north have acted as a planetary paving machine, covering impact craters with billions of years of lava flows that created the large smooth plains existing today.

Many Martian craters are named for famous scientists or astronomers, but some have been named for literary figures associated with Mars, including fiction writers H. G. Wells and Edgar Rice Burroughs.

26. MARTIAN DUST STORM

The Martian atmosphere is much thinner than that of Earth. The atmospheric pressure and density are 100 times less than our planet. This thin Martian "air" is composed of 95% carbon dioxide, 3% nitrogen, 0.13% oxygen, 0.03 water vapor, and a trace of other gases. Even if the atmosphere on Mars contained the same proportion of oxygen as earth (20%), it would be too thin to support earthly life forms. There are three types of clouds visible in the Martian sky: dust clouds, frozen carbon dioxide clouds, and clouds of water ice.

Although the planet's atmosphere is very wispy, surface winds that can reach 350 mph regularly cause major dust storms. They form mostly in the southern hemisphere during the summer months and lift the powdery surface dust high into the Martian sky where it may remain suspended for months at a time. The surface of Mars is covered with a finely ground mixture of silicon dioxide (sand) and ferric oxide (rust). When the *Mariner 9* space probe reached Mars in May of 1971, it found the entire planet enshrouded in a global dust storm.

27. *MARS OBSERVER* SPACECRAFT, 1992-1993

Beginning in the 1990s a new wave of Mars-bound robot space-craft were developed and launched by NASA/JPL. The first of these was the *Mars Observer*, launched in September of 1992. It was designed to orbit Mars and study global geology, gravitational and magnetic fields, and atmospheric conditions. It reached Mars in August of 1993, but contact was lost with the spacecraft short-ly before it was to go into orbit around Mars. Investigations have since determined that a catastrophic explosion caused by a fuel-line leak or over-pressurized fuel tank either destroyed the craft completely or sent it spinning out of control into space.

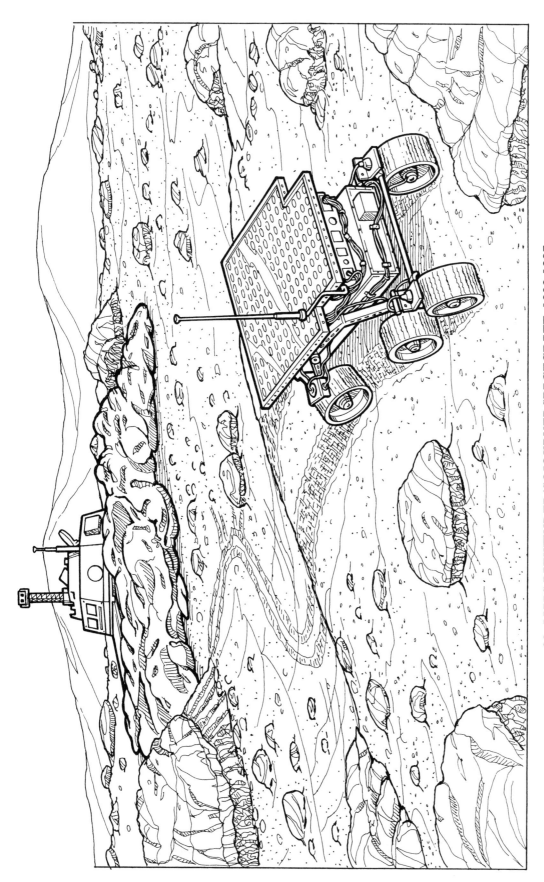

28. MARS PATHFINDER/SOJOURNER SPACECRAFT, 1996-1997

The most ambitious and successful Mars exploration spacecraft to date is the *Pathfinder/Sojourner*. Launched on December 4, 1996, the robot probe consisted of a mother ship/lander, *Sojourner* (top), and a detachable roving vehicle remotely controlled from earth, *Pathfinder* (bottom). The two machines reached Mars on July 4, 1997. Entering the Martian atmosphere at 16,000 mph, they were protected by a heat-shielding aeroshell, slowed down by parachutes, and encapsulated in an inflated air bag similar to those found on automobiles. The air bag absorbed the shock of impact on the surface of Mars, then deflated. *Pathfinder* opened up its four petal-like solar panels, allowing *Sojourner* to roll onto an ancient flood plain in the *Ares Valles* region of the planet.

The stereoscopic TV camera mounted on a telescoping mast above *Pathfinder* provided the first-ever 360-degree panoramic view of the surrounding Martian landscape. The photos revealed a terrain composed of large and small rocks, gullies, hills, and two mountain peaks in the distance. The six-wheeled *Sojourner* began to explore and examine the area close to the *Pathfinder*. Its spectroscopic analysis of the rock formations indicated that they had been swept to their present locations by an ancient flood, confirming scientific theories that Mars had once been a much warmer planet with abundant surface water. This discovery is also supported by recent photographs from the orbiting *Mars Global Observer* spacecraft showing ancient water-gouged river channels on the Martian surface. The *Pathfinder* landing site was named the Carl Sagan Memorial Station, after Dr. Carl Sagan, astronomer, writer, and advocate of Mars exploration.

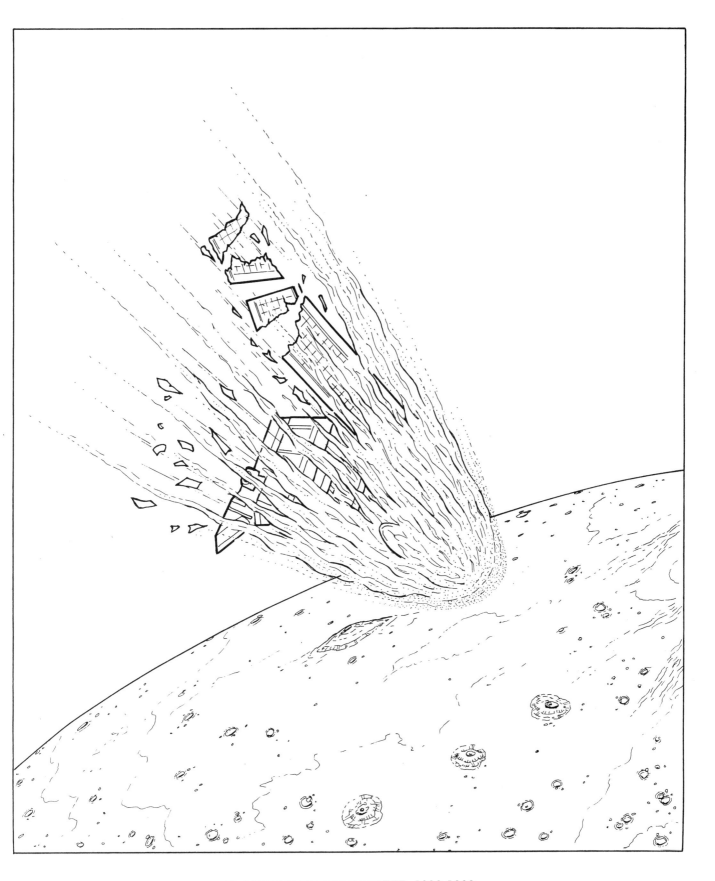

29. *MARS CLIMATE ORBITER*, 1998-1999

The next in the series of robot space probes sent to explore Mars was the *Mars Climate Orbiter*, launched in December 1998. It was designed to orbit the red planet for two years, mapping the entire surface with the highest resolution color photos ever obtained. Unfortunately, like the earlier *Mars Observer*, this spacecraft was also lost as it was about to orbit the planet in September of 1999. An error in navigation caused by faulty conversion from the U.S. standard to the modern metric system of measurement is the suspected cause of the failure. The fate of the *Mars Climate Observer* was most likely that it either overshot the planet entirely, wandering off into space, or that it approached Mars too steeply, causing it to burn up from friction with the atmosphere.

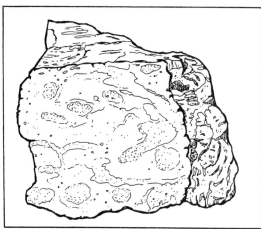

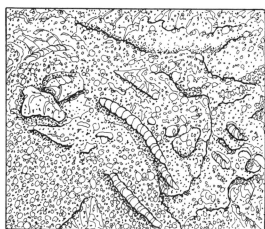

32. MARTIAN METEORITE ALH 84001

In 1984 scientists made a remarkable discovery on the frozen ice fields of Antarctica. A rocky meteorite found in the Allan Hills region and dubbed ALH 84001, was determined to have originated from the planet Mars. It began its earthward journey about 16 million years ago when a massive asteroid collided with Mars. The impact sent billions of tons of rock into the Martian atmosphere and outer space. Drifting through interplanetary space for millions of years, the rock was eventually captured by Earth's gravitational pull, falling to Earth in Antarctica 13,000 years ago, and not discovered until 1984. The meteorite was put aside for later examination.

In 1996, the 4.1 pound rock was cut in half and subjected to close scrutiny under an electron microscope. Scientists discovered what appeared to be evidence of fossilized microbial life forms, in this case organic molecules called PAH's (polycyclic aromatic hydrocarbons). These can be created in only two ways,

either by the biological activity of microorganisms, or in the planet-formation process. The way in which the molecules and fossilized worm-like structures exist within the rock strongly suggests a biological explanation. Different scientists have taken opposing positions and the subject is still an open question. But it seems highly likely that if Mars was once a warmer, wetter planet as all the investigations to date suggest, life forms may well have developed there, as they did on Earth.

There is also a credible theory within the scientific community that meteorites from Mars may have "seeded" the ancient lifeless Earth with microorganisms that traveled aboard these rocks. Over billions of years of bombardment by such meteorites, Martian life-forms may have begun to flourish when the climatic conditions on Earth became more hospitable to the evolution of life. If this theory proves true, then humanity is the ultimate progeny of our long-dead Martian ancestors.

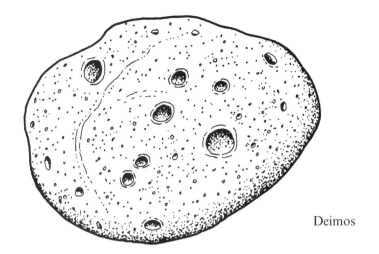

Deimos

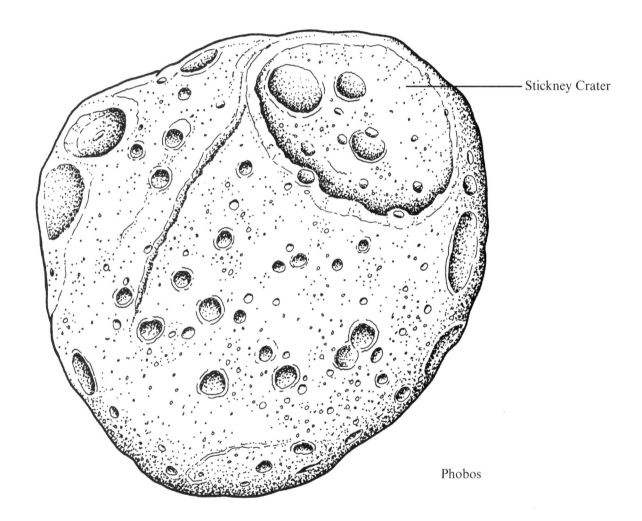

Stickney Crater

Phobos

33. MOONS OF MARS, *PHOBOS* AND *DEIMOS*

There are two small, potato-shaped moons in orbit around Mars. *Phobos* (Fear) and *Deimos* (Flight) are named after the servants of Ares, Greek god of war. American astronomer Asaph Hall discovered the two moons in 1877 while working at the U.S. Naval Observatory in Washington, D.C.

Phobos is the larger of the two satellites, measuring roughly 13 by 17 miles. It orbits Mars at the relatively close distance of 3,700 miles. Deimos, on the other hand, circles the planet at a

distance of 14,500 miles; its size is about 6 by 10 miles. By comparison, our own moon is 2,159 miles in diameter and orbits the Earth at a mean distance of 238,000 miles.

Both Martian moons have craters, cracks, and fissures covering their bumpy, uneven surfaces. *Phobos* has an especially large crater named Stickney, evident in the above illustration. It is about six miles across. *Deimos* is composed of extremely dark material with a very low albedo (degree of light reflectivity).

34. *MARS ODYSSEY* ORBITER, APRIL 2001

Shown above approaching the red planet is a robot probe launched in April 2001. The *Mars Odyssey* Orbiter reached Mars in October of 2001 and went into orbit around the planet. It is designed to map the surface using a high-resolution camera and infrared thermal imager. It will also analyze the mineral composition of the planet's crust and search for hydrogen in the sub-surface area. The presence of hydrogen is one of the markers that would indicate the existence and location of water on Mars.

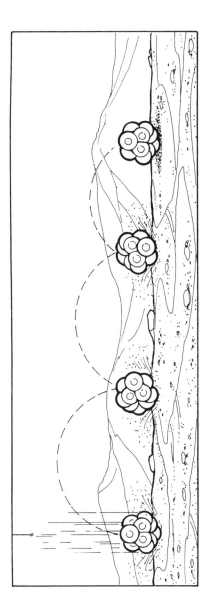

35. MARS TWIN ROVERS, 2003

Next in the continuing series of Mars-bound robot spacecraft are a pair of large mobile vehicles, the Mars Twin Rovers, destined for launch in May and June of 2003.

Both vehicles are identical six-wheeled machines designed to wander over the Martian landscape at different locations on the planet. They will carry more powerful and sophisticated instruments than the *Sojourner* rover of 1997 and be able to travel 110 yards each

Martian day, farther than the *Sojourner* covered during its entire 100-day mission. They will reach Mars in January of 2004 after a seven-month space journey, descending to the planet wrapped in the same type of shock-absorbing air bags as the *Pathfinder/Sojourner* lander. The rovers will analyze rocks and soil to determine the climatic conditions of ancient Mars. They will search for signs of early life and for the presence of water both past and present.

36. FUTURE MARS ROBOTIC EXPLORATION, POST-2005

A variety of proposed Mars robot exploration missions have been suggested by NASA and other space agencies. Jacques Blamont, a French space scientist, conceived of a Mars roving balloon mission, depicted above. Filled with hydrogen gas, the balloon is designed to descend close to the surface during the cold Martian night and rise again when heated by the morning sun. Blown by Martian winds, it might travel dozens, or even hundreds of miles. A tether line suspended from the balloon would carry instruments to analyze the soil, while a camera took close-up photos of the landscape. Although an innovative idea for observing large areas of the planet, no further development work has been done on this concept. NASA's Ames Research Center recently proposed an idea for low-altitude flying above the surface of Mars. A sophisticated model airplane, remotely controlled and powered by an electric motor, could observe and photograph dozens of square miles of Martian terrain.

Other new Mars missions are currently in development. These include another orbiter with powerful photographic and radar imaging capabilities for 2005, a complex roving science-lab vehicle in 2007, and several soil-sample return missions scheduled for post-2010. These efforts are all in preparation for the greatest Mars exploration adventure ever, a manned mission to the red planet by the year 2020.

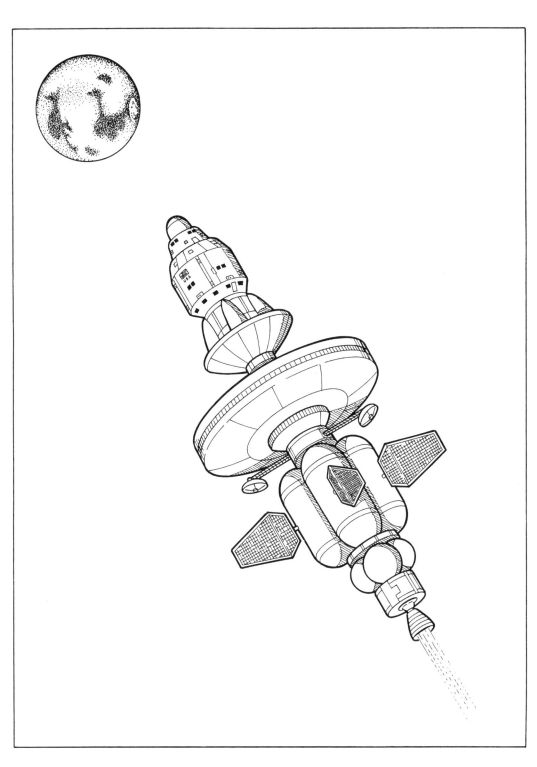

37. MANNED MISSION TO MARS, 2015–2020

The most exciting space voyage in human history could well occur within the next twenty years. Present NASA plans call for a manned spacecraft to land on Mars sometime between 2015 and 2020. A possible scenario for such an expedition would begin with construction of the Mars spacecraft by astronauts working from the orbiting international space station. Pre-fabricated components would be ferried up to the final assembly point near the station. Astronauts would fit the pieces together to complete the ship. By starting their Mars journey with a ship already in space, the enormous amount of fuel needed to escape the earth's gravity would be conserved for the Mars flight.

One possibility for such a spacecraft is illustrated above. Its sections might consist as follows (from back to front): engine exhaust thrust nozzle, engine components and combustion chamber, propellant tanks, movable solar panels for electrical power, steerable radio antennas, a spinning center habitat disc to provide artificial gravity during the long space voyage, a specially shielded chamber for crew members to enter during solar storm radiation flare-ups, a heat-absorbing aeroshell for descent into the Martian atmosphere, the landing/ascent ship with extendable legs, control cabin, and descent parachute nosecone. Using propulsion based on current chemical rocket technology, such a ship would need fuel, oxygen, and supplies for a six-month spaceflight to Mars, a year-long stay on the planet, and a six-month return trip. Breakthroughs in engine technology such as ion, plasma, or nuclear propulsion could shorten that space travel time.

As configured above, only the landing/ascent portion of the Mars ship would descend to the surface of the planet. The mother ship would remain in orbit waiting to reconnect with the lander after the Mars exploration mission was complete. The landing/ascent module would serve as the crew habitat during their exploration of nearby Martian terrain.

38. ASTRONAUTS EXPLORE MARS, 2015–2020

NASA is considering several different mission plans for a manned Mars expedition. In addition to the single spacecraft proposal previously described, a multiple-ship program is also under study. This would entail launching an earth-return ship first. It would remain in Mars orbit fully fueled and provisioned, waiting for the astronauts to link up at the end of their mission. A cargo and habitat lander would be launched next, containing all the supplies and fuel needed by the explorers while on Mars, as well as an inflatable habitat structure to house the astronauts. The manned Mars ship would be launched last, reaching the planet after a six-month flight and landing near the pre-positioned base camp. After completing their Mars exploration, the astronauts would enter an ascent craft, designed to rendezvous with the orbiting earth-return vehicle. Most plans currently under consideration call for the Mars astronauts to remain on the red planet for a lengthy stay of between six and eighteen months.

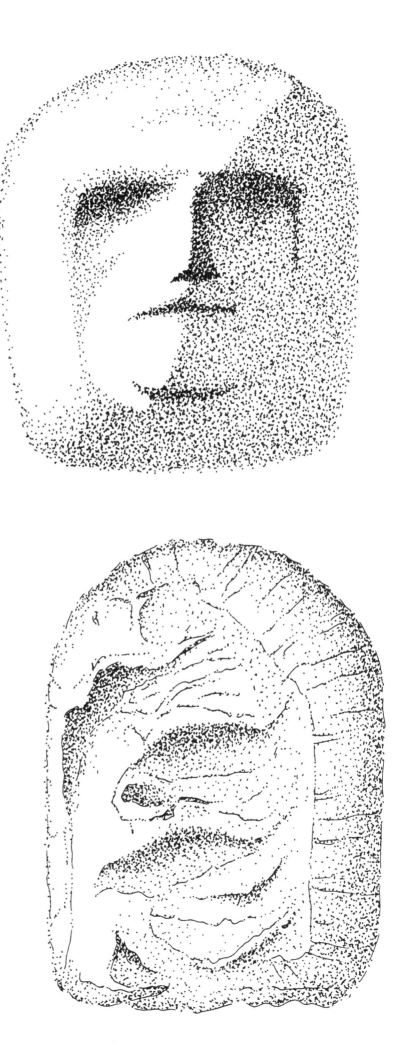

39. "FACE ON MARS" MYSTERY

During the *Mariner 9* and *Viking Orbiter* missions of the 1970s, an unusual rock formation was photographed in the Cydonia region of Mars. It has become known as the "Face on Mars" due to its resemblance to a gigantic, helmeted human face. Some serious scientific investigators have studied photographs of this area and believe that it is an artificially built structure over one mile long, a mile wide, and 1,500 feet high. They have also observed triangular structures nearby that resemble pyramids. Could this be an ancient Martian city centered on an immense monument? The photos have raised speculation and debate about this possibility within the scientific community; however, most experts discount the idea. The *Mars Global Surveyor* spacecraft currently orbiting and photographing the red planet has added support to the view that the "face" is a natural geological formation.

In April of 1998, the *Surveyor* passed over the Cydonia region at an altitude of 270 miles, taking new photographs of the "face." Taken at a different angle from the earlier photos, the new images show a distinctly natural-looking hillock or knob with gouges and bumps on its surface. Staunch believers in the "artificial-construction" view claim the new photos have been altered by NASA to hide the truth. Eventually, astronauts will solve this mystery when they explore the site in person. The question of whether an ancient Martian civilization constructed a gigantic monument will finally be answered.

40–41. ASTRONAUTS EXPLORE MARS IN ROVING VEHICLES, POST-2020

As subsequent manned Mars missions are undertaken, more permanent habitat structures and additional equipment will be needed. In order to explore Mars fully, the astronauts will use vehicles that can transport them to locations many miles from the landing site. They will be able to investigate and examine the rock formations, valleys, gullies, and dry riverbeds that cover the surface of the planet. Many scientists believe that permanent colonies of Mars researchers will be established between 2050 and 2100 A.D.

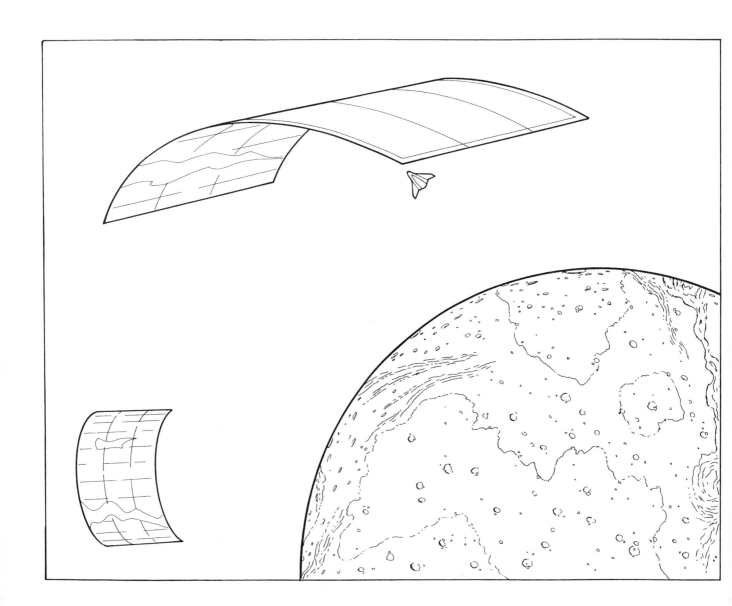

42. MARS TERRAFORMING BEGINS, 2100 A.D.

When science-fiction author Arthur C. Clarke based his 1952 novel, *The Sands of Mars,* around the notion of transforming Mars into a habitable planet, he provided the spark for the idea of "terraforming." This concept is now a valid theory, considered well within the scope of present and future technology. It will be a long process, however, taking several hundred years to complete. The first step in the endeavor involves increasing the surface temperature of cold, dry Mars. Many ideas to make it a warmer planet are being considered. One plan is to place enormous mirrors in orbit around Mars (see above). These would gather and focus heat and light from the sun and reflect it down to the surface of the planet. Another idea calls for covering the

bright white polar ice caps with a dark soot-like material to absorb more of the sun's heat.

The most effective method for raising the temperature of Mars is to increase the amount of "greenhouse" gases in the atmosphere. These gases, principally carbon dioxide and chloro-fluorocarbons (chlorine, fluorine) would create a "greenhouse effect," trapping the sun's heat in the lower atmosphere, and preventing it from radiating back out into space. Warming Mars by these methods would release sub-surface frozen water, allowing liquid water to exist on the surface. This water, along with the increased temperature, would facilitate cultivation of green plants, the linchpin upon which Mars terraforming hinges.

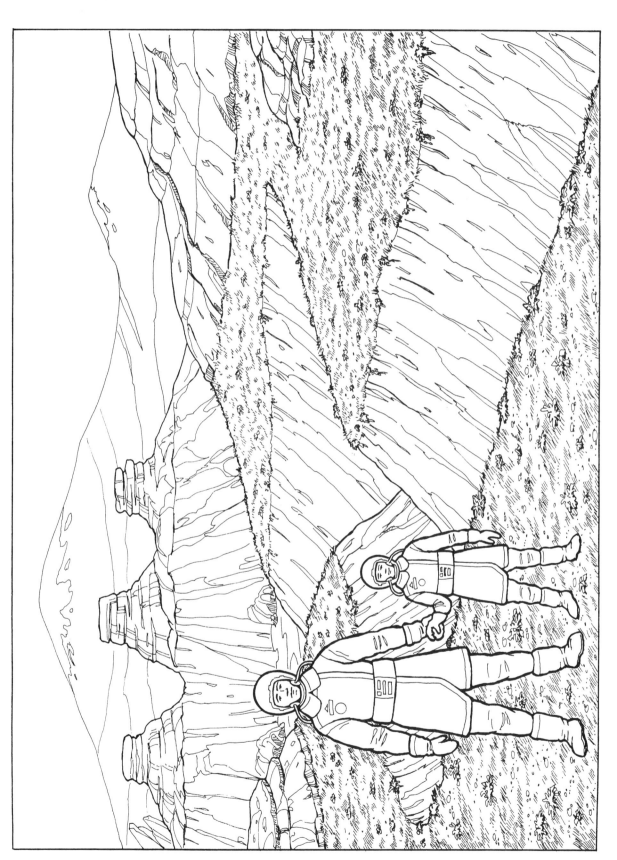

43. GREEN MARS, 2100–2200 A.D.

The relationship between animals and plants on earth is "symbiotic" (mutually interdependent). Animals, including humans, breathe in oxygen-rich air and exhale carbon dioxide, while plants take in carbon dioxide and give off oxygen. The key to making the atmosphere of Mars breathable is to increase its oxygen content. This will require large-scale cultivation and growth of plant life. As equatorial areas of the planet become warmer and wetter, green plants will flourish and the oxygen content of the atmosphere will increase. However, to provide a breathable atmosphere may take 100 to 200 years.

44. BLUE MARS, POST-2300 A.D.

It is possible that within the next 300 years, Mars will have been completely transformed into a warm, wet planet totally suitable for human habitation. As the temperature increases globally, large quantities of water will be released onto the surface, allowing for greater areas of plant growth. More plants will provide a thicker oxygen-rich atmosphere. Lakes, rivers, and even oceans of liquid water may eventually develop. Perhaps then, Blue Mars will join its sister planet, Blue Earth, as a home for human life in our solar system